PANA⌐⌐

POEMS FROM THE TOWER POETRY SUMMER SCHOOL 2009

*Edited by Jane Draycott and
Frances Leviston*

OXFORD
TOWER POETRY
2010

CONTENTS

Poems from the Tower Poetry Summer School 2009

BETH AITMAN

Forest Man

In the sound of a leaf in the wind, you're followed;
there's a face, twilight-blue in the gloom, made of bark
and oak leaves and ferns, you can smell the pine of his skin.
In your run you hear his footsteps crackling, see
sudden moonlight in his eyes, thousands of him behind trees.

Back home, safe in concrete and sturdy streetlamps,
there are still thickets of people in the streets, in alleyways
men whose faces are twilight-blue, with skin like bark.

The Key Kitchen

This is the place keys are made.
It is cavernous, and dim, brimming with heat,
full of steam and smoke that shrouds the workers
so they are only shadow puppets, who brew
and mould and make. It smells of wood,
and copper, and hidden things.

They make huge iron keys
to throw into the sea, to rust,
to shut great doors forever.
Silver keys, for secrets,
with twisting teeth that tarnish.
And tiny crystal keys, simple and glittering,
cut from quartz: to hold close,
or someday give away. They shatter easily.

At every fire, metal is changed and cast
and cooled into mysteries: keys for gates
and dungeons and cities, keys for the depths
of the earth and keys for the sky.

The Village

Even the hills are sleeping. Their quiet limbs flow down
to a village drowned in dreaming, too lazy to wake.
The open roofs of houses sit in sad gardens, choking creepers
draped over trees. The people sleep, in creaking beds
or on the street where they stopped, overcome by doziness.
The church's half-built spire sags, moulting loosened bricks.
People do not leave this village of idleness, cursed quiet,
rolling through decades, ungrowing,
in sleep which is a kind of gentle dying.

BETH AITMAN is 18, and currently reading History at St Hugh's College, Oxford; until now, she has lived in London all her life. She began writing poetry almost accidentally at school, and has now progressed from limericks and miserable sonnets about being a teenager to something that is hopefully a bit better and doesn't make readers want to tear their eyes out. After the dreadful sonnets, she has mostly given up on rhyme except as a practice exercise, on the premise that it is amazing in the hands of people who can use it properly, but she can't work out how to make it work yet. She is still trying. Having not done English for A level, she now regrets this simply for the missed opportunity to come across many more poets than she's had the chance to; however, her other A levels, particularly History and Biology, crop up frequently in her writing. Hopefully these give different perspectives on what she tries to achieve in her poetry, particularly using scientific vocabulary and concepts to explore aspects of the world which aren't so scientific. Failing that, she at least gets to use pretty words like haemoglobin and osmosis. Her favourite poet at the moment is Louis MacNeice, for far too many reasons to list, but particularly for his effortlessness in rhyming, and for the last poem in 'Autumn Journal'. In her spare time she doesn't do very much, as work, rowing and sleep take up more time than actually exists in the week; if given the chance she does like baking inadvisably complicated cakes and attempting to play the guitar. She had better go and write an essay now. She hopes you like her poems.

JAMIE BAXTER

At Your Bedside

The trick is to talk about normal things
how the kids are getting on, the view

but the kids hardly ever come
and the sky's a restless hue

it's strange that in such godless places
we sit so solemnly on our pew

you tell us about your newest pain
but this is all I do:

wonder how I would cope
if I were as ill as you.

Farquhar Road

Slip past the gate: half down,
Half up, given up like most.
Weeds tear through gravel,
Moss swallows brick.
Reclaimed before its time – and savaged.

Evidence of human hands near-gone:
Someone near-death not left in peace
But preyed upon.

        Not even memories
Aid but rather depress, as at the top
Of the drive the house seems unsalvageable.
Utterly lost in itself.

        Rather than the past
The future is before us: the house is gone,
The ground eyes the sky, the bricks build something new.

Bluebells

Two boys circle him,
the gravel grinds under their feet.

He carries bluebells, those risen up
through the undergrowth. He worries.

How often she had walked that wood,
loved those flowers growing wild.

And how he now regrets dropping them,
kicking out,
         running home
the gravel soaring up like hope into the air.

JAMIE BAXTER is 20 and has been writing poetry for four years. He is in his second year at Durham University studying Engineering. He read at the London Poetry Festival last August. He has been recently published in *Pomegranate*, *The Delinquent*, *Spark Bright* and on the website of *Read This Magazine* as well as two Durham University publications *The Grove* and *Forced Rhubarb*.

I think I really started writing poetry when I started reading it critically. Not the handful of poems in an English GCSE anthology but collections such as *Crow*, *High Windows* and *The Waste Land*. Following on from this initial exposure, the poets who inspire me now include Don Paterson (It's not the lover we love, but love / itself, love as in nothing, as in O;), Wallace Stevens (We say God and the imagination are one . . . / How high that highest candle lights the dark).

My poetry always seems to revolve around the human experience: how we interact and react to our surroundings and experiences. This means I often engage with nature but only as a metaphor, I hardly ever look at nature for nature's sake. I've been told I'm obsessed with my own mortality and I think this often comes through in the themes I deal with, such as illness and death and also themes including the search for knowledge and love, a pastime which is always left half-finished.

Studying Engineering and having not studied an English A-Level I often worry about how 'qualified' I am to write poetry. However, as I continue to read widely and form opinions on poets and poems I feel like I am growing as a poet. I always try to have some sort of message in my poetry, like a story to be learnt from or an observation I want to share. And this is the kind of poetry I like, poems that chime with my thoughts, or take my mind somewhere new: to an idea I'd never have considered or a different view of an experience like love (Paterson's *My Love*) or death (Larkin's *Aubade*).

When writing I normally start with an idea, a first or last line and see where they take me. The poem often changes completely from the first idea, but this is almost always a good thing.

ALEXANDER FREER

Petit Saut with Persian Rug

A clutch of red wires or filaments
meeting a thousand others in the fabric flesh
solid and rough in red and gold recess
of the carpet on which we walk.

Play through these moves *andante*,
a ballet for four feet, parting the
floor. Our flaw in this is shuffle-play:
we step aside to block one another.

A careful choreograph perhaps
incorrigible, our performance
is variations on a theme
like dust in the upper atmosphere,

a momentary touching,
a friction of particles beyond control
before they are consumed
in red and gold.

Commute

We went by train that day, it was
busy so I sat facing back,
watching new stops, bricks and hedges
not appearing, but peeling away.

You wouldn't think it so important,
taking the opposite seat. A snug binary
rarely causes concern, save for
the text beneath the text,

the strokes of paint exhumed
from beneath the surface by x-rays,
the proof of our authenticity
in the reverse view.

In my new seat I read.
Make me ex-canonical for a day,
dwelling in the apocryphal,
which catches the light at this angle.

In the inverted library the ashamed
gospel is proclaimed: that other
passionate kill, the hot silver touch,
the glowing spear, my guilty ear,

the agony in the garden
writ backwards to heaven,
a man's predicted guilty touch
now the firm proof of piety.

All bets are off,
all odds are on,
the dark redeemer
is herself redeemed.

Spanish Song

Although you were fleeting like a flower's momentary exposure
I shall not make you a flower.
Although you were bold like the first spoken words
I shall not make you a word.
Although you held back like the sunrise on a November morning
I shall not make you a sunrise.
Although you blossomed within me like the stems of a poem
I shall not make you a poem.

ALEXANDER FREER studies English literature at Warwick University from where he edits *Angelic Dynamo* magazine. He is interested in research in poetry, critical theory and interdisciplinary fields involving literature, philosophy, psychology and biology. In his spare time he plays the trumpet and enjoys modern classical music and the countryside.

───────

Like so many people born in the second half of the last century, I was drawn to poetry along the axis which stretches back from T.S. Eliot to John Donne. Travelling from Eliot to Whitman and thence Hart Crane, I came to Wallace Stevens and lately Geoffrey Hill. It is in Hill I find the poetics with which I most firmly identify right now. It is power and richness of the verse which appeals to my sensibilities, as with the music of Shostakovich or Philip Glass. I am interested in biblical verse and epic poetry, but like any person alive today I can only access such texts through our prism of romanticism. In the Hebrew bible and the great epics I find an aesthetic of violence which is terrible and sublime. In Hill this is married to a gifted lyricism of the calibre I first experienced in Rilke. I am not ashamed to admit backwardly it was then after Hill that I learned to be astonished by Milton. To circle back to where I began, the poetry that I have found the most powerful to read is inevitably the sort of poetry I want to write.

It has been said of Robert Frost that he focused his poetry on only the great, serious issues of life. If I am being immodest then I regret it, but I feel that in a brief stay of existence, it is only logical that I should find these great matters the worthy subjects of poetry. I cannot escape Whitman's verse-promise to 'never again mention love or death inside a house' because that would surely be the death of poetry, and Whitman must have known it.

EMMA JOURDAN

Body

Each time the morning grazed your face
there was less of it left,
drinking mud until the mud and you
were hard to tell apart.

It shaded your eye sockets,
your whole flattened brown head,
your necklace of tiny bones.
It warmed your skin, and after that was gone

it cooked you till the meat of you
was brown and hard. You lost your legs,
fingers, half of one arm, and your face
became mud-smooth, eyeless.

Still – most of a leather belt, a bracelet,
strands of brittle hair – milk and wheat
in your stomach – you don't seem
to have lost so much. Really you're lucky,

because we're pulling out hard cylinders
of mud from incisions in your thighs,
chest and throat,
holding them up to the light

of yet another morning. Because the mornings keep coming
and people who see you now look away,
walk out of the room,
touching their necks, staring at the floor.

Seeded

The seeds were ferried across in bottles,
and found their way
to the shop round the corner.
You'd snap off the lid,
tip seeds between your lips,
gobble them like water.

They were red and shiny,
traces of juice still on them. You licked them clean
so no one would see –

what did you think we'd think?
Seeds, maybe hundreds,
swimming in your gut, your blood, your brain,
burrowing. Of course we noticed.
They flushed themselves through you.
They reddened your skin. They showed
behind your teeth when you smiled.

When you fell over
what spilled out looked almost solid –
your forehead spitting out seeds into our hands.
Then we'd wipe them off, and put you to bed,
watch you reach sleep
while they squirmed under your skin.

Lockstitch

I'm as straight-laced as the corset you wore
for your eighteenth birthday,
trailing blister-coloured ribbons down the hall.

What do you want me to do about it?
You can rub me up the wrong way,
knit your fingers into my scalp
and press your mouth against my hair

but it's all dead cells you're touching
and if you keep staring at me
as if you can see what's going on –
the laces knotting in my head,
and sewing machines pricking out a pattern
of tired yellow fretting fraying strings –
I will be too scared to speak at all.

EMMA JOURDAN is 19, currently studying history at Oxford, and lives in London when not at university. The writing started when I was about five or six with four page novels in which people I didn't like were eaten by dinosaurs. After that there were twenty page poems in which every other word was usually either 'death' or 'alone' and paragraphs of solid text contemplating the meaning of life. What I'm going to write about now I'm not really sure yet; I like personal and confessional poetry but I think I'd like to get outside my own head for a while. Which is easier said than done, but studying history, especially when it comes down to thinking about how disappeared cultures thought and worked, is starting to give me some ideas.

———

Favourite poets is something else I'm not sure about. I haven't actually been reading poetry for all that long; I really like Philip Larkin, Don Paterson, Louis MacNeice, Paul Muldoon, Bernard O'Donoghue and Colette Bryce at the moment, but I change my mind a lot. I always like people who can do things I can't – like use rhyme brilliantly or write poetry with a political edge that doesn't sound preachy – but ultimately I think my reasons are mostly emotional rather than rational. Which in a way is something I like about poetry – it has more direct access to subconscious thought than prose does, I think, mostly because of the importance poetry puts on sound as well as meaning.

SOPHIE MACKINTOSH

Pavor Nocturnus

Heart is a bird again. It flickers
against my ribs. Outside
there is a streetlamp: its light
washes out my unfamiliar skin.

Soon it will be busy. Sirens will sing
blue into the air. I will be dismantled.
The trace's horizon will needle at the beat,
my clockwork will be probed - this is what happens

once you've kissed someone
under a bulb's flare, and let them open your bones –
the nurse raises a vein. And look how
the electrodes sear, like fingertips, against skin.

Barbershop

Yes, my love, keep the scissors sharp.
The hair in the eyes stings like vinegar.
It falls in sheaves. *Tell me*
the story of your mother's funeral
(and the blades, they flicker their wings
about your head).
Tell me of your father lathered up in soap.
The razor's sweep: flinch. The bathroom tiles swam under
the light, and he had forgotten
his face. He found he looked like you.
(And the locks cling to the carpet as though burred,
and you sit as the towel is beaten out).

Winter 1995

Before the New Year we ran away
up the Gurnos, where boys with fresh toy guns
fired them into the air. The houses
were dark and laid out
like teeth in gums.

From the roundabout you could see
the fake mountains, rising into the sky.
Coal dust bled out from under the grass
and saplings. We pulled them up.
Their roots were white as bone

but my shoes stained black. Sometimes
snow covered the heaps of waste
so the landscape was, temporarily, perfect.
We slid down them
on tea-trays, table-cloths, rubbish bags.

Gurnos = the Gurnos estate in Merthyr Tydfil, South Wales

SOPHIE MACKINTOSH is 20 and lives in Pembrokeshire, West Wales. She is a second year student at the University of Warwick, where she studies English and Creative Writing. She came third in the Tower Poetry competition 2007 and this was her second time at the Summer School.

I write a lot about small events, things from my own experience. At the moment childhood is an interesting theme for me as I am almost twenty-one, and therefore starting to look at events from when I was younger from a more adult perspective. My father is a doctor while my mother is a nurse so there are always books and magazines about illness around, which is something that fascinates me, and something that crops up occasionally in my poetry. Although I am studying English, science has always appealed to me. I thinks sometimes this relates to my writing style, which I try to make fairly precise and sharp, although I worry it can seem sterile at times. I want to be able to conjure up an exact image with as few words as possible.

One of my favourite poets is Eugenio Montale as there is a beautiful concision in his descriptions, yet he manages to get it spot-on. Another favourite is Paul Celan for similar reasons and for his incredible imagery. The writer who probably has the biggest influence on me is Angela Carter, with her way of finding beauty in the grotesque, and the richness of her imagination. Music and film are also influences, especially the albums 'Moon Pix' by Cat Power and the film 'Valerie and her Week of Wonders' by Jaromil Jires, which manages to be both visually stunning and incredibly disturbing.

The process of writing something, for me, is generally haphazard. I rarely write on paper first unless I have to as I get frustrated by how slow my hand-writing is. A poem will often end up being a completely different poem as I chop away at bits, rearrange, and rewrite obsessively, often spending half an hour or more agonising over a single word. There are countless folders on my computer stuffed with sentences and stanzas that have been amputated, or poems that have been abandoned. I am disorganised but I am also a perfectionist.

Jazz, in a Place they Wouldn't Normally Have It

The clash-trip of notes
from the sax player
is poetry; he
scratches your history
into the air -

and strings lick around
the room, unhinging
you from yourself. The

blue jazz bounces
down narrow alleys -
the buildings cusp and
embrace the sevenths

and the seconds of silence
that make a song what it is -

the bass player walks you to the future,
so be kind to this man with the red tie.

mirror therapy

we are a mechanical accident
looking at ourselves
naked in the mirror for
the first time since. It says
this is who you are.

she looks me in the teeth
and I remember to
stare straight ahead
like the last time I saw my brother.

it draws on bruises below the eyes
and leaves streaks in breath that tell
you that only your body will heal,

that the fallow earths of love and ache
make the soles bleed and crack the knees;
because hearts don't break -
they beat the shit out of you
and only your body will heal.

mercury

asthmatic,
every attempt at raising the
sails in this conversation.
in each other's image
we nail the tongue
through the jaw.

windows
grind in the walls
cracking
to give something
to talk about

and you seep in
like mercury,
risky and hot -

say
anything

SUZANNE MAGEE is from Belfast, where she studied at Queen's University for an English degree. She is a keen guitarist and in her spare time continues personal studies of Zen and jazz bass.

First and foremost I write about anything which urges me to, on paper/ post-it notes/other flat surfaces. I'm quite interested in the musical texture of words and sentence structures, and non-traditional verse forms.

I like writing in exploration of different structures of both form and theme, and sometimes write in an exercise of trying to create an image or experience through a piece of writing.

I'm influenced by my interest in the human condition, natural phenomena, the psyche, and most often, by personal experiences.

Cartography

I draw whirlpools in the sea and little
dragons bellying the peaks. And how I love
the inks: the scarlet, the blue, the green,
the black, the wicked gold. They make me
think of a purring decadence, which releases
itself from each delicious fold.
        And the tiny storm-spun
ships. I pass my fingers over the sails; I push
them round the ocean and into cliffs –
or, if I am feeling generous, into mermaid coves,
so those girls can practice on the sailors.

Giving these to you was almost an accident
(*or rather, lending. I want them back. Learn*
by heart or trace them onto your eyelids.
I'll grant you the time). How surprised I was –
you can read: you aren't confused
by the language used, or the keys etched
down the side. So I'll concede and draw
a path through the craggy passage, the woods,
the gorge, the desert, the mire. And place clues
along the side: you can collect them and know
what is right – the silk flowers, the ribbon
which threaded my waist, the heeled shoes.
        Find me
even when you trawl through Russian poppy
fields, and your head is drugged and drowsy.
A red line will always end in a garden. I'll be in
blue (carefully demure; feeding the sparrows).
Open your palms. See if they rubbed dark with ink.

The Fig

Choose, then bite. I've broken
the skin (*a blood-heavy bruise*),
which was beautiful –

and so, wouldn't this be quite the tragedy
without these pink seeds to expose – ?
They shine as secrets might:

deliberately catching – like hooks –
at vanilla flesh (*the lining of this womb*).
Folding the fig's core – the dark syrup

which preserves the kiss: a primitive
strain; no longer in our exchanges,
but wholly practiced among the trees.

I watch the walls of the purple sac
collapse, despite the attempt
to sustain these jammy eggs,

which are treacle-yolked
and somehow already embryonic.
Golden fish-eyes: they appear

sugar-blind and immune to separation.

Moon through Your Window

Pierce my finger: I know my blood would
be white. I should write blanched love-messages
on the glass – backwards, of course, so you could

understand (*although you would see*
anyway. What have you not known before?)
And the clouds strain the mixture: a constant

fountain, a wound in the sky – but bleeding
milk and muslin and herbs, all wrapped up
to make some sort of tisane, a poultice.

Is it meant for me? I lie under glass,
listening to a breath which is not my own.
The moon: she has a nun's face. I never

thanked her for her presence, for reminding
me of those who went before: so many.
Rosemary beacon – your dumb tenderness,

and your milk spun through glass, kissing
my hair, my throat. I can't hear my magpie
anymore: did it drown in this moon? The thumb –

crushed leaves and stems; the liquid welling up
as a dent in wet sand might swell up again
with water, then spill back into itself once more.

ANNABELLA MASSEY was a commended Foyle Young Poet in 2006 and has been published in *Pomegranate* and *Cadaverine Magazine*. She previously attended Sir William Borlase's Grammar School, and is now in her second year at the University of Warwick. She is reading English Literature and Creative Writing.

My poems start in notebooks – just as quick phrases, fragments or images. I work with these ideas (this is usually slow), and when I feel a more definite rush of thoughts and words, I'll move everything over to the laptop and keep up with this flow by typing. I often write about my own memories and experiences, or the process of communication with an object. A set of maps, for example, or a fig. These are very much seen and told from my own perspective: my poems don't directly set out to pursue or confront wider human concepts and universal ideas, though these might find their way in naturally. I almost always start with myself and develop from there – perhaps because I feel this gives me more authority and license when dealing with the subject.

I am not especially concerned with realism – I will distort fact or create an improbable landscape if this works to the poem's advantage. Recently, I used an exaggeration of the doppler effect, with an image of a red sky: fallout from the stars. I studied Physics at A-level and often make use of what I learned then. I like to work in form, but I also like to conceal this and wrap structure up in free verse.

I've noticed I address myself a lot, splitting in two. Or I use 'she'. So there is often a kind of internal dialogue in my poems. Sometimes, I can be hesitant about explicitly using personal detail and memory, so I might mask this with a series of images. But I would like to concentrate on developing a clearer, more economical narrative voice – I particularly like Margaret Atwood's. And I also like to experiment with and vary my tone, perhaps using italics, spacing and parentheses to emphasise these shifts. In general, I try to take example from Zoë Brigley, Sarah Maguire and Marguerite Duras, who I am reading a great deal of at the moment. And I have always read and re-read Wallace Stevens and Pablo Neruda, along with many others.

ASHLEY MCMULLIN

Compost

Emptying the caddy, I saw remnants
Of the last few days join the rotten pile
Built from months before: the watermelon
Slices from a birthday slid downwards, while
Newspaper tears - the US election -
Fluttered, fighting the forceful pull of time
Before falling, to join that old mountain,
Stinking and forgotten, we call the past.

Paper Planes

In class, once, we sent a paper plane back and forth,
Carrying messages, jokes and love letters,
Paperclips, pens, pencils, and toy soldiers too.
Once, after History, we planned the Greatest
With stacks of paper,
Reels of sellotape
And six weeks' hard work.
We'd set off for our fancies:
Egypt, America - even the Moon
Was etched on our desktop universe.

In class, today, I made another;
After several corkscrews and
A dip over the teacher's head
It crumpled, smudging false borders
Of Ancient Greece, and falling
To join the dust,
With all the other dreams
We'd once carried.

The Veteran

These clothes, they don't fit me no more - too bright,
too smooth, dressing this dry and paling skin.
These eyes, when I look, don't have that same light
now, like they used to; the places I've been,
the bright bars and coloured nightclubs, tonight,
all the pretty people, faces I've seen
and cocky kids I swung at, don't seem right.
Earlier, I could feel myself dying
as I waited in the kebab queue,
seeing - in the mirror - the fresh, lying
clothes . . . not seeing the old self I once knew.

ASHLEY MCMULLIN is a 1st year undergraduate currently reading English at Christ Church, the home of Tower Poetry in Oxford, having completed the IB diploma at Colchester Sixth Form College. His poem 'Journey to Hilly Country' finished runner-up in the 2008 Tower competition.

———

Ever since an early age (pardon the cliché), Ashley McMullin has been a keen writer, from childhood yarns to the most dismal attempts at sincere prose. And yet, it is only very recently that poetry was introduced within his creative spectrum, a newfound indulgence he owes largely to the discovery of Philip Larkin in sixth form. His poetry orientates itself subsequently around metre and rhyme, opting more for a traditional carriage in which to transmit modern-day thoughts and experiences, perhaps occasionally dwelling on the meaning of life, as you do. His rewarded performance in the Tower Poetry competition has spurred him on to further exploration of his poetic scope, though prose remains his favourite medium by which to channel a strong, long-standing motivation for written expression and storytelling. The works of Joseph Conrad, Gerard Manley Hopkins and Miroslav Holub, amongst many others, have been especially influential and inspiring to Ashley in his appreciation of writing and its place in his life. He is wishful that his penning skills may come to serve wider, beneficial causes later, with future aspirations based in the professions of journalism and teaching English abroad, following on particularly from involvement with the campaigns of Amnesty International during his time at college.

Alongside the writing, interests such as travelling, music, football and pubs have all constituted a major part of Ashley's everyday existence, which has lately lead him to Oxford University; born in Colchester, he spent his life growing up in Essex and now splits his time between his native, eastern home and university life in the west. Whilst studying at Oxford, Ashley hopes to significantly extend and build on his range of reading and writing, and can regularly be found (if not by the bar) tackling an essay in the Bodleian Library.

PAUL MERCHANT

Peru

It is not that late. An ascending line of globes
oranges the street. Phone wires hang,
like in Westerns at midnight.

Above, the roundest moon I've ever seen
dangles, ready to drop like a marble.
It is bluish-white, hypnotic. I could be here an hour

or longer and longer

Distance

A painted village
fused to the bank
drifts by, in brushstrokes.

You love France like this, even when
a race against a thunderstorm
forces forgetfulness of colours.

Nothing but the time remaining,
limbs burning, glass currents wrenching
you to the bank, the reeds,
(cloned, brittle reeds)
and tears and rain on brightened cheeks.

After, it is nearly comforting
to find a kayak lying empty,
like yours, blue plastic among plants.
No energy for back-story. Nothing but gazing
at crystal distance, the sky now reddening.

1925

Arrived Tuesday 9pm, on the clipper "San José".
While docking at the port, I saw a man
on a pier, shifting on boards, then falling.
Those behind attended to their boats.

A ride to the centre revealed shops
thrown together from scrap and logs
and plastic labels, selling rice next to tools.

People walked by open drains
in one sock, no shoes, or with just a glove.
They shouted or whispered, depending on the second.

A curious thing: the city lies
on valleys of a steepness you or I
would find insane. Young and old
climb and descend with disregard.

I didn't wait to be invited
to enter someone's house, just asked:
there is no yes or no, just shrugs.

An armchair blocked the only door
so I squeezed, as they do, through the gap,
found on the floor a man extended,
grey, freezing, nibbled by rats.

I pride myself on cultural knowledge,
and fluently asked: "A burial rite?"
I received a shrug, and sat cross-legged
by the dead man, in order to write things down.

PAUL MERCHANT was born in 1991 and grew up in Surrey. He started writing poetry at 13 after the encouragement of teachers at his school, and has been doing so sporadically ever since. He won 3rd prize in the 2009 Tower Poetry competition, and his work has been published in *The North* and in *Pomegranate*. He is currently studying French and Spanish at Cambridge.

———

As far as I can see, writing poetry takes a certain amount of bravery, in which I often find myself lacking. The bravery is in ignoring the little voice which tells you "it's no good, this is terrible, why even bother?" It is also in convincing yourself that you have something worth writing about. I often wonder where (if at all) one draws the lines for subject matter in poetry. Much, or even most of what I read seems to be based directly on personal experience. There's no doubting that it is a mine of powerful images and feelings – perhaps the only way to achieve authenticity. However, I now think that to make use of it, the poem doesn't necessarily have to talk about it. I have recently written poems which are more imaginative, even fantastical. Nonetheless, if they work at all, it is because parts of them are based on things I have seen or done or heard.

Other than that, there is little process to my writing. It is rather more erratic than I would like it to be, mostly because I often have to force myself to sit down and do it. Once I get going, there are usually interesting words to be written, but I'm not at it all the time. Some of my best ideas come to me in the shower, which is not hugely convenient for recording them.

As well as struggling to sit down and write, the other great battle I have is with form. While I don't agree with Stephen Fry, who seems to think that if a poem doesn't conform to traditional structures or meters then it is worthless, I do believe those forms have real value. Still, up until now I have written nothing more advanced than a sonnet. Villanelles, sestinas and the like elude me. That is perhaps the next goal.

AMELIA PENNY

Snow Day

This is an unseen picture:
She had lost the day in sewing: gardens, fishponds,
Swifts in the eaves,
And he in hefting cold black soil
In sacks through the house, for the spring.

He took out those old films which were
The evidence of what we had once been. The screen
Lit up like a small dawn window among stacks of papers,
Sewing thread and unused colour film.

The snow was walking its wide shadow
Like a pale pigeon, all along the greenhouse roof,
And the sky was focusing its blue onto
Our side of the boxed pearl of the world.

The dusk seeped out from underneath the paving stones.

They watched a small boy wading
An Atlantic shore, or striding a cold tideline in bright boots.
They sat like a Flemish portrait as the slow
Submersing snow climbed over the cold windowpanes,
The sharp box hedge, the tender ice-shy ferns.

Belt

That thing over there, that dull crude mass
Of rain and grass and dung – give me its skin –

And so the light came in. It took itself
From the salt and the slither of knives,
And was a fine thing – polished, weighted, stamped
With cost and quality –
It took one shape, though would have taken any.

It has known a life of partings since, and each time fallen
Calling brass-mouthed for its creature. Each night
Hung like an arm looped over a backrest.
It was discarded for its grease, its sweat,
Its water marks – almost a hide again.
No second tanning works them out, no cleansing.

The Painter's Pigeons

Sunlight is the life of us,
And it draws voices from the small wells of our throats
Like a pump draws water. Gifting us our shadows,
Those rare figures in this attic junkshop.
It is then that all the bars come off the world
And we are spoken to in nonsense.
We are held in a loving fist.

We all dread rain, when we are lustreless
And when for days we watch our wheatseed
Creeping into leaf, our water clouding over.
We stay silent. We know where we are
So well that we have been released, and come back to our cages
Hungry, thirsty, unpreened. We have seen
That outside is all roads and rooftops, slack grey water.
Dawn is just the slipping of the cloth
Down from the big blue birdcage of the sky.

AMELIA PENNY was a runner-up in the 2008 Tower Poetry competition, commended in the under 18s category and winner of the under 14s category of the Stephen Spender Competition. She has lived in London all her life, and is studying Natural Sciences at Cambridge.

———

Nature is probably the biggest theme in my poetry, and my interest in it is also the reason I study science. The natural world is a place where both art and science have something to say, and I enjoy combining their different ways of understanding it, as I believe that this is the best way to appreciate its true richness. I don't set out to write 'nature poetry' as such, although I do admire the work of nature poets such as Ted Hughes and Gerard Manley Hopkins. It's more the case that my own interest in nature means that I tend to at least consider it in the course of a poem. The question of where we stand in the natural world interests me, and it surprises me that we so often see nature as simply the 'everything else' in the world which is not directly related to ourselves. The more one thinks about nature, the stranger it seems that we have chosen to draw this line, and the more imperative it is to question our reasons for doing so.

My writing process is quite disorganised; once I have an image, or an idea, I write a page or so of notes relating to that subject, very quickly, and if there's nothing that interests me on it, I usually give up and move on to something else. If the result does interest me, then I'll immediately work it up into a first draft, which I will then forget about for a couple of weeks and rewrite a few more times. I once saw an interview with a guitar maker on television, where he said that the secret to making a guitar was to take a bit of wood and cut off everything that didn't look like a guitar. That's more or less the attitude I take to writing.

LESLIE SMITH

For Want of a Garden
for Annie

You are the one I always go to. I look for care and understanding
as I would look for a dress: rarely, but fervently on the occasion.

You know me the best. I have watched you become happier
than you imagined, and I have heard you as you walk

through life as a series of open rooms, each that pleased you.
I walk parallel, meanwhile, where there are no windows,

and when I stop it's to ask you about the garden,
my face pressed to the gap beneath the door.

I see your feet, springing and turning. I whisper,
"Tell me about the stems. Tell me about the webs."

You say it's a garden. Mysterious to you why I cannot find it, why
some of us walk like caged things and can see no views,

scrounging for stamps of light, information and grammar.
I wish you all the leaves in the world.

Underground

Pressed, back like a leaf to carriage roof, feeling cobalt
bumps and bricks pushed against the grain of your fingers:
plasterwork bite one,
                    three,
                        six nails. You cannot take your hands away –
as if gaping at the surface of some closed underwater world,
nymphen-tide brought home and homesick to your concreteness.
When and why does your world invert? Does it matter?

Deserts of sugar cave for gravity but salt constructs: crystalline
and as threaded to your palmlines as the light at the end of under.
If you take your hands away, now, from the frozen,
cup wounded fingertips in like a snail,
what else will you feel but the sting?

The Compulsive Liar

In the tree after carefully climbing up,
balance and see the prize:
opportunity guised in porcelain blue,
speckled with briar to warn, but you take it.

The nest falls groundward – no putting back the egg.

How to climb out? How to climb down? You'll need both hands –
can it fit in the cradle of your teeth without breaking?
Yes; to swallow is to smash so you climb out, climb down,
push aside consequences though they're there.

But even when you find the nest,
replace the egg,
consider all amended and walk away –
what happens then?

Left, it will eventually be eaten,
or it will grow, birth, crawl but not fly
until you're found and to sate it teach it
as only you can – more eggs.

LESLIE SMITH was born in Louisiana, USA and spent the period 1998–2009 in England, where she completed her BA Creative Writing at Bath Spa University. She will be exploring other interests such as dance, photography and psychology while her writing develops further. She writes poetry and prose under the pseudonym Taegan Harker.

Leslie draws on her experiences as an expatriate in particular for her poetry, something she avoided for several years until encouraged by her mentors on the BA – she has Tim Liardet, Carrie Etter, Gerard Woodward and Greta Stoddart to thank for her progress thus far.

Her poetic influences include Li-Young Lee, Molly Peacock, Alice Oswald, Joel Long and Michael Ondaatje as well as her writing peers, although a rhythmic background in dance and a love for music are also heavily present. Having grown up in the Deep South, with its rich mix of cultures and rhythmic way of speaking and living, Leslie enjoys coming to music and a sense of religiosity through her poetry. She is very fond of experimenting with wordplay, form and sound, and sees poetry as a means of embracing, enhancing and capturing synaesthesia. For her, poetry is the portrait of a moment.

Favourite themes include misconceptions, spirituality, personal darknesses and beauties, and Leslie's own experiences of loss, love and travel. After so long shying away from the confusion brought by her double-life as American-born and British-taught, she is finally learning to embrace the edge this brings to her observations and metaphors, and use them as a platform from which future writings can grow.

TESS SOMERVELL

Panado:

A roulade of herbs and tortilla chips,
a smack of spice,
baked in a flat, round pan.
It is also
a garden party.

Here the panado dish is traditionally consumed.
The garden is rather a yard,
flat and round like a pan,
a dusty yard in the shade of a still pinata.

But it is also
a dance, which takes place at the panado.
It kicks up the dust,
stepping and pounding,
hissing and spitting.
It makes up a little for the stillness of the pinata.

Panado is
the quality required
for dancing, eating, attending the panado.
That is to say it is
bravado,
and panache.
This is the most important panado
on which the others depend.

Panado is
furthermore
the courtship
that inevitably follows
panado of any description.
It tastes like tortilla, is bright like pinata,
it unsettles the dust,
and is typically brash,
steamy,
and brief.

At Silver Heights

after the painting by Lionel LeMoine Fitzgerald

Eights trees; one woman; innumerable clouds.
But they are not separable.
Each cloud could be a hundred other clouds.
That branch could be an arm, those ankles could grow straight
    from the earth.
Beyond these clouds + these trees + this woman
there are textures + countries + orange + sex.
But here is a woman in pink, resting her arm on a tree.
For her the space is still like a sky.

Pineapple rockets

Environmentally,
and economically,
like space travel
pineapple
ought
to be a rarity.

It ought to be a luxury:
the gold and juicy
rocket ships
of stacked rings
a status symbol
how high you can go.

If you get
a whole fruit,
a whole spiny planet,
complete
with crater skin
and leaves
like volcanic eruptions,
and the gumption
to be so ostentatiously Hawaiian
in your kitchen,

then you know
you've made it.

TESS SOMERVELL was a winner of the Foyle Young Poet Award in 2006 and afterwards co-founded *Pomegranate*, for which she is now Art Editor. She is studying English at Christ Church, Oxford, where she has edited poetry for Cherwell and acted as President of the Oxford University Poetry Society. She was awarded the 2010 Lord Alfred Douglas Memorial Prize for her poem 'From Mary Spencer to George Stubbs'.

———

I'm never conscious of a personal 'style' when I write poetry, but looking back over poems I've written certain themes do tend to crop up: food, nature, the countryside, and – so I've been told – sex. If I start writing without knowing where I'm going, it inevitably ends up being about cows. I'm apparently drawn to vital, sensual themes and images, but I like to think there's some philosophy going on there too. If there is it usually appears afterwards, after I've done the vital, sensual stuff. Then I read back and think, 'oh, look, there's some epistemology in there', or whatever. I don't know if it's wholly accidental, or whether one half of my brain has been working at something in the same poem without the other half's knowledge. Either way it does make the writing process exciting. There's always a surprise at the end, even when that surprise is just some more cows. When I'm reading other people's poetry I like to wonder how much of that poem's meaning came from a conscious decision on the part of the poet; it's impossible to tell. The same goes for all my favourite poets, from Colette Bryce and Paul Muldoon, down through Elizabeth Bishop and John Donne to Chaucer. And I wonder if we appreciate how lucky we are to have such a completely free and infinite resource like language.

SOPHIE STEPHENSON-WRIGHT

Gibraltar Rock

The Barbary apes are gawping
at tourists, slouched
on the low-stone wall;
making snatches at sunhats

and camera straps, they watch
the sun-creamed strangers
scuttle past.

It's just before noon
and a love-sick swallow stalls
on the Upper rock;
stopped-off
on the long-haul
to Africa.

He sizes up the distance;
sees an empty stretch of sea-breeze
and the continental gap.

The warm sea bumps
at the hot-rocked harbour;
a dot-of-a-boat is pulled
with the swell of the Straits

and somewhere
alone on the Rock,

an old man sings to the fish
as he guts them,

watching the sun fall away
from the sea.

The Square Mile

It is late September and
the afternoon is early.

The pigeon-wings
beat lullabies
in time with traffic

and the mirror-buildings rest,
all straight-edged glass and
holding the sky in their eyes.

You watch
as a cloud drifts past
on the seventh storey;

a man looks out
from an office window,

parts clouds
as he blows on his coffee.

Alone On A Wide Blue Sea

I used to fly in planes
over a wide blue sea

and it was just me
and my plane, and nobody else
but the butterfly birds

and the big black whale
I'd sometimes see singing
to somebody else.

Once, the sky slipped
under my feet,
staring back, sulky;
watching my belly
all wooden and white

and the clouds hung up;
like fish underwater
they'd float to the top,
belly-up

and I felt the sea
falling, down from above
where the sky should have been.

SOPHIE STEPHENSON-WRIGHT is in her first year at Oxford studying Biological Sciences. In 2008 she won the Ted Hughes Young Poet Award, and was one of fifteen winners of the Foyle Young Poet Award. She has been published in *Pomegranate* and was shortlisted for the Christopher Tower Poetry Prize in 2009.

———

There are lots of young writers who have gorgeous, distinct styles to their work, but I'm not entirely sure that I've managed to find mine yet. When you take part in a workshop or writing course, you find yourself at the end of it with a heap of work that is all very different in form, content and style, and I find this is the case with most of the things I write at home as well. I think it is important to give yourself the freedom to have a go at things; to write both short funny poems and long lyrical ones, to rhyme and to use form and to play around with words. I wouldn't say I had preferred themes – I think there are only so many times you want to explore something before you get bored and have to move on – but certainly I steer towards the more visual end of things. For me, I write as a means of taking the pictures in my head and putting them into words.

I always write first drafts by hand with a pencil and notebook; whatever I can think of, I just write it down. The first draft may get changed a little bit, but I often try to keep moving forwards and get things out on the page. Once I have a full-ish length poem, I'll type it up and make bigger changes – changing words and lines, cutting stanzas. This is when lots of re-ordering goes on, but also quite a bit of new material is written (often to replace or fill in for the sections that have been cut out). I try and save drafts once in a while so I can get things back in case I regret deleting something, but it's also quite handy for looking at the progression of a poem as it develops. Most of the time, I'll also print poems out and make annotations and changes in pencil again, before going back and doing a final edit on the computer.

IONA TWISTON-DAVIES

Night Dust

Your desert has a skylight
that opens onto night.
Feel yourself bake.
Feel the sand clutch your bare feet
And reach

You can't see the white planets
just behind the frame
or the paper tear comets
You've only got your sand
And your now imperfect blue.

There's a sideways pillar of cool
you can step in and out
and the sand plumes
and gets stuck in the sky.

Doesn't it appeal?
Aren't you going for the glitter
and the shock of black?

Brace yourself against the skylight's sides.
It can take it.
Jump and fail.
Jump again.
Take the heat and use it
Use it to get to the speckled side.

The Silent Street Festival

Sleep-cycle through your streets.
The sudden cool veil
and the sound of sun on cement
are comforting.
A lone jogger envies as you float past.
Somehow there is no separation
between machine and thoughts and destination.
But waiting around the
corner poised
straining to shout surprise is
a festival blossoming six feet over the street.
Where the trees' soft fingertips
are your tarmac aisle's confetti.

Running From Bones

My father lit little fires on the cusp of the woodburner
to please his bones.
My legs appreciate the blaze but it burned
so fast collapsing into
eager ash skeletons
as I hurried from the house.

*

The watered up sun is helping
as I'm dashing past traffic radiating
Hurrying to meditating.
To the gardens.
In the sketchy grass,
collect a grip.

**

Crease the features.
And soon start making sense
of why I charge as if chased
and my haste from the house
as my father's bones creaked.

IONA TWISTON-DAVIES is 18 years old, comes from Oxford, but is currently living in London studying English at Goldsmiths College. She has been a writer for most of her life, but never tried poetry until she heard about the Christopher Tower Poetry Prize. She's very grateful for it.

It's difficult to explain my writing process; it depends upon the type of poem I'm writing. Some of my poems are about real situations I've been in when I've seen something beautiful or strange or slightly frightening. I'll come up with a small phrase to describe it and build a poem around that in my head on my way home. Then there's always a desperate hunt for some scrap of paper I can get it down on before I forget it.

Other times, I have an idea and I just sit down and play around with it on the page, scrawling multiple poems in all directions with my pen. Then I'll come back to it later and sift through for the best images to put together.

Either way, writing is a fairly instinctive process. Like a lot of people, I use it to vent feelings, or gather my thoughts, or just to preserve a time that was special to me. I often find inspiration in the world around me, sometimes nature, and sometimes people. To me, writing always feels like an important act. You're creating something permanent with the power to affect people, and unlike so many other things, you can say it's yours.

I'm pretty new to reading poetry, but I do love e e cummings and T.S. Eliot. The instinctive, beautiful feeling of a thought process is absolutely stunning to me. But I don't think I can claim to be inspired by them. I don't read poetry whilst I write and I find it easiest not to think about anything at all. I think the relationship between my writing and reading is that one is always an escape from the other. If I have to write an essay, I'll take a break with a book. If I'm rushing to finish reading a text for a lecture, writing is always there tempting me but calming me down.

Beth Aitman

Jamie Baxter

Alexander Freer

Emma Jourdan

Sophie Mackintosh

Suzanne Magee

Annabella Massey

Ashley McMullin

Paul Merchant

Amelia Penny

Leslie Smith

Tess Somervell

Sophie Stephenson-Wright

Iona Twiston-Davies